Wind
of the
White Dresses

WIND

OF THE

WHITE DRESSES

MEKEEL MCBRIDE

CARNEGIE MELLON UNIVERSITY PRESS
PITTSBURGH 2002

ACKNOWLEDGMENTS

The Author expresses her gratitude to the editors of the following
publications in which these poems first appeared: *Agni Review*:
"Strauss and the Cows of Ireland"; *After the Storm*: "The Intention";
America: "Lake Meadow Sky"; *Boston Review*: "Contents of a Breath
About to Be Exhaled as 'I Love You'"; *California Quarterly*: "In This
Moment","The Ghost That Every Night Gives Birth To";
Caprice: "North, Late April", "Dare", "Having Become Aware of
Certain Things"; *Conscience*: "Weather Report"; *Georgia Review*:
"To the One Lost on the Other Side"; *Grand Street*: "This War"; *New
Virginia Review*: "The Gift", "The Angel in the Cereal Box"; *North
American Review*: "All Hallow's Eve"; *Passages North*: "My Friend,
Lost to Me in the World", "Why I No Longer Have to Eat"; *Seattle
Review*: "The Whole Weight of It"; *Seneca Review*: "The Tree of
Life", "Good, I Said"; *Southwest Review*: "Window"; *The Nation*:
"Miraculous Shrine of the Stairway Dime"; *Virginia Quarterly
Review*: "Dreaming Space Awake", "Some Kisses", "Interior Painted
on a Blind Eye".

"All Hallow's Eve" appeared in *The Best American Poetry—1992*
edited by Charles Simic.

CONTENTS

1 WISHBONE

2 WINDOW

for Lysa James

1
WISHBONE

A FEW LITTLE KNOWN FACTS CONCERNING THE POTATO

*

Long before Buddha or Allah or Jesus
appeared on this earth
there was the wild potato.

*

The potato makes its living
by doing translations:
mud into food, dark into light, stone into soul.

*

Huge white palace at ocean bottom where passengers
of the Titanic arrive alive, intact, white pearls of their happy breath
forming the potato's pure heart.

*

The potato is the soul's twin, mute, complete, not nearly
as solitary as it first appears.

*

The bones of the potato are made of rain.

*

The potato is the only living being that wakes and dreams
simultaneously.

*

St. Valentine prayed in private to certain lesser known
varieties of potato:
Ox Noble, White Kidney, Early Rose, Ringleader, Flourball.

*

The human dreaming of the potato
dreams of eternal life
while the potato dreaming of the human
experiences only the strange,
salty taste of the finite.

*

The only god the potato believes in is the shovel.

*

The eye of the potato
is not so much a matter of vision as it is the lover extending
a humble bouquet to the beloved. That is, earth.

*

Little Columbus from the dark interior — the potato
divulges another part of mystery's map,
another intimation
of the new world, each time
it is brought out of earth
by your hunger.

PHYSICS

The interior
of my body's all galaxy. If you could open me
you'd find
a hut lost in deep forest
glowing with candle-bouquets

the beggar the hermit the witch
left in the lonely room — stars
I saved from the long trip here. Home
through the red meteor shower of early July;
home through the moon's white door.

Such a fine skein of music and skin
seals from sight all this dazzle.
Do you suspect I am making this up?
Why do you think I have never let anyone see me
sleep? I will let you.

Breathe stars with me as I sink into a boat of light
so deep and sweet and wide
that even the most innocent witness
finds the entire blue weight of earth
forcably an interior treasure.

My soul's such a glitter even sunflowers
in fields hundreds of light years away
lean and dance in my direction.
You say *a conceit, a fantasy.*
I say *physics.* I say *solar wind,*

the secret sheen of my clean blood
and bequeath to you
my life. In passing, I will
not spill skyward with my blue suitcase
of meteors but sink inward

like sequins falling from an opera gown
into a city fountain, like the tiny island
of light a lost coin makes as its tumbled
into deep ocean. Evidence
of me will remain

though perhaps undetected.
My story is your story. Your story is a tear
that breaks free, shooting star, sequoia:
all night, planets scattering
through random branches.

NORTH, LATE APRIL

Public radio. The announcer,
Mozart-rinsed, means to say,
In the North, flurries expected
to fall but says, instead, *flowers.*
Before he can correct himself, look —
there they are! roots down, petals
pluming out in parachutes
on a rescue mission: irises
that recall the twilight violet
of Cleopatra's eye, the same
blue of her deep Nile,
then freesias, tulips, daffodils
and a red can-can of azalea.
This cold and leafless place
petal-assailed, saved
by the mistakes desire makes.

THE MIRACULOUS SHRINE OF THE STAIRWAY DIME

Fourteen wooden steps to my front door.
On the fifth step, a dime that's lasted there
for years despite dust and brooms, boots that ferry in
mud-lumps and lakes of melting snow.

Finally, to celebrate, I tape next to it
an antique post card: St. Anne de Beaupre, a blue
robed, hand-tinted virgin — she has to be a virgin
in a dress that blue, holding aloft

a little man in pink pajamas and this, of course,
is Jesus, gold spikes of light flying from him
straight and strict as a grade school teacher's
admonishments, or a father's: *Sit still.*

Stop singing. Now we will begin our sums.
But I climb past, thinking of my friend in seminary
how the dime would not be enough
to reach him now, how letting go means just that.

And where I see the miraculous star
of God's heart holding steady, I am afraid
he would describe a riot of blasphemy. But I know
this: as a child, he'd put his pillow

on the windowsill waiting
for the visitation of satellites
and shooting stars. How later, his mother
would smooth his dew-drenched hair then draw him

back gently without waking him
into the dark and starless room,
a child still shining
from the far worlds he had been touched by.

IT IS ORDINARY, I AM

awake though well on the way
through the secret door into sleep.
The one painted the same color
every night. But this time
I can see the start
of the world. That far back.
No *I*, just light, indigo
as a dragonfly's wing,
the blue of day but farther
back than that. No air,
no earth, no sun. Simply
the beginning. We are making
the world and there is only
one of us
though soon we will separate
into bodies just
for the joy of it:
anthracite, protezoa, tree frog,
human being. I am awake
in incorporeal levity as *we*
or *I* or that one in indigo
vertigo invents air to remind
my lungs of the blue treasure
they fill with, then spill
to you, who holds the gift
for a heartbeat before
passing it
into thrush's warble.
A miraculous alchemy
calculated into all of memory
shared equally —by breathing—
among priests half asleep
in the dark

confessional, husks
of deep-sea dreaming abalone,
the truth of it shining
even in a forest pebble. I was
awake but I did sleep later
because I could see how simple
it all was and I knew
I would remember.

AFTER READING YOUR POEMS

for Jay Apt & David Romtvedt

During the night,
the night I lost my human body, forced
to learn tunnel digging from the mole;
the night they smeared fireflies
into paste
for later use as iridescence
in the fabric of rich people's party clothes;
the night no one
was ever there again. That night,

you, whom I had never met, went out
with a simple hand-made basket
to save what you love
from this life, from this earth.
To me, much later,
it seemed you had been harvesting

stars, light from other worlds, slight
inscriptions, traceries of phosper
carried gently back
from the endless dark. It makes
me think of wild

blackberries retrieved from green caves
of roadside weed; blue river pebbles
in the hermit's palm
offering peace treaties to loneliness — how much
the life of every nameless
thing matters. I know an astronaut

who, flying through deep space closed
his eyes and found — glowing there — particles
of aurora borealis, his whole body

steeped in it. Now, like everybody else
he moves through grocery stores
and cinemas. Ordinary

scissors cut his hair but he has been changed
in a way not even he can describe and what
was given to him cannot be
taken away. It is the same
for me after reading what you wrote.
You simply stood

all the darkness someone else
might have died in, keeping your hand open,
and what light you saved, you passed on
willingly. I am writing to let you know
I received the gift and to thank you. How many
wishes have been granted, how many souls

reborn in just such returning light.
Every single bit of it glad and true
as those birthday candles that don't go out
no matter how hard human breath
assails them. The joy from this: paperwhite
bulbs that have waked

indoors, whispering their Buddhist prayers
into pure white petals
while outside, the November wind
tries to erase
from the world every warm thing
and, happily,
fails.

HALF-TREE WOMAN

I may look like a tree to you, arms raised
as if beseeching the horizon to stop swallowing
sun whole. But I am something else.
I am a woman safe enough to hold still.
Family to wind. Dark as the inside
of a chiming clock at dusk.
Like Lot's wife, I turned to watch
the cities of forgetfulness burn and stopped here,
rare spice, a woman whose tears left
weeping's harvest visible. Green, ripe, I take root
deep as words in a lullaby.
Clouds spell their dream alphabets through me.
I extend myself into the world first
by dreaming — green needles stitching nothing
to something: breath to wind,
wind to underwing of red-tailed hawk,
hawk shrinking to black star
over the open field — forging light
from the furnace of its golden lungs.

TO THE ONE LOST ON THE OTHER SIDE

When you drown I pull you from the lake
and breathe into you a knowing
until you rise, flame, into the sun's
luxury of ressurection,
until you spill home again, unlikely, alive,
orphan of the hourglass.
I scratch your story into a bar of soap
then wash my hands, as Irina taught me.
So I will remember.
So it is not written.
So there is no evidence to be used
against. I will step in front
of the bullet for you or the knife, stand
whole as the bone noose of a hand
closes at my throat. I have done this.
I will do this. I will be
a sundial bleached white
while the prophets preach heat, preach
flare, teach the blue
chastity of flash fire. Your life
lived in secret, a hut of ice built
on even thinner ice and the thaw coming.
Come home with me. I will feed you. Here is clean
water, the wishbone. Here are some black plums.

*Note: Irina Ratushinskaya was held in solitary by the Soviets and
forbidden to write. She scratched her poems with matchsticks on
bars of soap, memorized them and then washed her hands.*

2
WINDOW

WHY I NO LONGER HAVE TO EAT

Where the ache was
and then
the emptiness
I planted
a field of sunflowers,
that is,
in my stomach.
Why not? Fertile
ground. Sky
infatuated with fol-de-rol
clouds. A riot
of rain. Just enough
room for the tiny
farmer and his red
tractor. Even room
for the millions
of ants, their love
songs and black
suitcases.

NOT ONE BIRD IN THIS

Sun's gone. A black-necked goose swallowed it
and went south while I slept. All right.
That is the way things are.

Perhaps later darkness will alter
with January's glass moon, full of the gifts
lovers, during the lost years, could not offer.

Open my diary if you wish. You will find
only white petals spilling
from that cramped little apartment. Imagine!

For years now I have been sending you
love letters written on the snow's pale paper,
written with ink of the after-midnight wind.

DARE

Just as what remains of harvest
sinks back into earth,

just as the dull worm curls
into the palace of an apple,

one thousand infinite winds
issue their invitation to the burning.

In coats of cacophony
a few fat crows accept,

strutting straight through
October into winter

on the raw dare *come
as you are*, perfectly aware

of how their feathers
will glow:

black lanterns
against the coming snow.

ALL HALLOW'S EVE

A mouse
gnaws a hole
in the white grain sack of sky.
Night spills everywhere.

Small ghost
racing for a hiding place

but only fields loom up
wide and starless and low.

Knotted tight
at wrist and neck —
the dirty bed sheet

she will have to live in
for as long as red leaves fall.

And what costume
is *he* wearing this time —
Raphael, Lucifer,

father? Tall as the balding
moon, he splits
a doll's face

as he steps near enough
for the flames
stitched into sour wings

to scissor
their golden tips deep
into his daughter's
lamé skin.

WEATHER REPORT

Local wind moves the moon
slowly up and farther away.
Knuckle bone of a drowned child.

THE OLD BLACK HAT

Huge hand
of the night-cloaked man
pulling out of the old
black hat
rabbit after rabbit.
Ears stretched taut.
No tear ducts. I hoped
there was a small farm
backstage,

the animals allowed
to sleep in real grass;
bouquets of lettuce
set before them
every morning, fair pay
for the wearing work
of making magic. My mother
wore dime-store pearls,
peeled hard berries,

shine gone,
the seed part intact.
I would burrow
in her closet,
the green evening gown
buried so far back
in the dark its fabric
was nothing
but hiss, scratch and old

perfume. Sweet to live
in her abandoned
clothes. My brother and I
walked with handmirrors
held to our faces,
a game we made
to shock away the familiar
walls and in
this backward vision make

new rooms bloom. I ate
soap and dirt and had
my own toy medicine
cabinet, tiny alligators painted
on the mirror. Black, faster
than a slap, rats shivered
through the backyard
where I played. Slash of sharp
teeth, rotten tails souring

the garden of old roses
no one bothered to water. My sister
wanted the door to our room
open. I'd wait until
I could hear her breathe away
into sleep then I'd shut
it, stare at the green
nightlight but the rats
still gnawed through, opened

our stomachs as we slept then ate
with casual, wide-eyed malice
the whole red mess. Once my brother
tried to burn down the house.
We didn't play in his room
much. The walls were yellow.
He wet the bed. It smelled
bad in there. He got hit
again and again.

He was so little. I wish
the house had burned. I was born
with a red birthmark
on my face and I thought it meant
I came from Mars
where all red things
came from: foxes and the ball
for jacks and certain special
dinosaurs and the flame

on the end of the kitchen match
my mother used to light
her cigarettes. My father
beat her, said he was going
to kill her so she took us
to a playground. We just sat
there. My brothers and my
sister. It got very dark. I thought —
if I don't move, someone

driving by will notice
and stop to help but no one
did. This much seems fair: to hope
the magician once loved
his rabbit. There is only one
although sleight-of-hand
sweeps it senselessly through
the same empty black hat into a mirage
of many, of family.

THE INSIDE STORY

Saguaro.
Thorn castle
of a forgotten
soul.

Inside this
cool ballroom
lizard child
grieves

while a blasé
sun in
monotone
repeats,

"Come lie down
outside
and I'll give you
sleep, sweet

as cinnamon, sleep
for centuries."
But in
saguaro

lizard
dips her feet
into a thimble
of star-chilled water,

readying herself
for the long
race across
fire.

THE GHOST THAT EVERY NIGHT GIVES BIRTH TO

Whatever the mushroom wants to punch through dust,
I am. Bed sheet, mourning veil, the ghost
that every night gives birth to. Heavy body
falling on me. City of resin. City of roses.

In all those places I was born and in all
those places on the edge
of the knife did I die. He was mountain. He
was air. He was sword blade, the fair wind

that sent the stricken sail boat home,
colors in him like the palette locked away
in the dead painter's tin box.
He was as lost as skin

from the shamed snake who slipped out
of the old life and stayed the same. Every morning
he ate live chickens, dice, whiskey
distilleries, the sun

but stayed so empty he had to eat his own children;
their smiles, guileless as xylophone music;
their toes, curled together like seahorses;
their eyelashes, delicate as the glass rafts of sleep.

He was crocodile, his maw
raw with the roses of a suitor. He was sweat
on the knife handle, stale salt
in a dirty sheet, the shout

of a man leaping free
of the bridge, as he did almost every night, falling
like a broken kite, shorn tail, shattered stick,
calling out, *You. You did this to me.*

THE CLEARING

Behind the house,
a few hag-scrappy forsythias.
The place raked leaves
were dumped and left
to rot.
Also, a ring of trees,
enough for me
to call
the woods
and go there
every chance I could

where an ancient man
once in awhile
would step out of the center
of a huge maple
and help
his equally
ageless wife
through a doorless trunk
into the small
dark clearing.

They never spoke,
never fought.
It was enough,
in a world
where there was no
place safe but here,
that they wanted to be
with me. He was thin
as wind. She always wore

a hood the same color
as sky.

If it was dark,
small lights
speckled the cloth.
If it was storm,
he could fly.
They loved me larger
than night and knew,
of course, the terror
our red house held.

It hurt them
terribly to leave
the center of the tree —
as hard for them to find
this world
as it would be
for a child
to try and push
a paperdoll
through an iceburg

but they were,
my memory tells me,
there, never
one without
the other,
more whole
than flesh and blood,
secular and
simple as the rain.

THIS WAR

Husband, the entire top
of his skull
missing in the last war

tours the liquor cabinet,
his cork screw poised
passionate as a Baptist minister

just before the sermon
while the bony wife's busy
sawing the newest baby

in half with a bobby pin.
I am not happy here. I have
never been

happy here and so slip
into the future like a bead
off a broken string,

simply another numb child
popped into the big suitcase
of bones

that an adult is.
Borrow whatever
spirits I can

from a bottle. At last,
glass home of my own.
Then one a.m. lawn-dancing alone

over pity-sharp stones
but sunrise, mother
of the little jewel,

arrives. "Look," she says,
"that is not a red shoe
on your foot.

That is a wound.
Wake up.
You are still alive."

INTERIOR PAINTED ON A BLIND EYE

Halloween, at the dry cleaner's, a young woman
bends over, mending something you can't see.

Straight from the nuns, Catholic kid,
at a black sewing machine, old fashioned kind.

Blind crow pecking path-edge for crumbs
the children dropped before they disappeared.

To her right, on a trellis of metal
the silk flower of a wedding gown rises out of season

waiting to be altered. What you see as you pass
the tiny shop: a full length skeleton — crepe paper crimped

into accurate bone — suspended just overhead on a shining hook,
waiting to be released into the empty dress.

Below, the girl stops to suck a bloody finger, just the one
you'd use to point out the way to any lost stranger.

WINDOW

What if it all goes away? This big wind
that's swallowing the yellow leaves — it's more
than a thousand sunrises to one tree alone. I mean —

what if the coat rack trees, skinny and empty,
what if they get swallowed, too? Roots, the last to go,
upended like great filthy wigs up and down this quiet street

and green lights and porch swings and the train's
long prairie-soaked sigh and from far away
the prairie, already covered with snow, swallowed

but not by wind because that would be gone, too,
and not into earth, either, because just dead people
full of blue chemicals are inside the earth,

wishing they could play poker or have a little drink
but they can't even clack the castanet
of a few freed-up bones. And all I can think

is how lonely this is going to be with the trees gone,
the faces and the trains and maybe what's left — just
the window I'm watching through and on the other side,

some rain coming straight down. That's all. Just falling.

THE GIFT

for Mark McCarthy

Once you told me how you saw angels sweeping over
this old mill town we both live in, meaning
pigeons, meaning you could see what was really rising
on such unloved and determined wings.

Now, from the only window where I live, I watch
hundreds of them lift from the slate roof of St. Mary's,
white ones in the middle; the others, gray
and clean as rain, range out, around to form

one huge wind-blown flower, a chrysanthemum of wings
from you, for me. But I have to go back in
to this house I'd thought was new and clean
and full of light. It isn't. It never is.

The high, smoke-blurred Victorian walls — thick with filth
from the basement butcher shop that nightly burns
body parts no one wants to buy. And even though
I have soap and paint, the walls in this waking dream

of childhood are never going to come clean. Then I hear
you, as if nearby, bemused that I have been so slow
to see. Leaning, leaning to me, you whisper,
"Don't you remember? Your soul is made of birds."

3
AZURE

THE INTENTION

We move into the field. Late summer grasses, gold
and high as our waists, open in the fragrance-soaked wind.
The man with me, a naturalist, says,
"Look. Two eagle feathers," plucks them up
then lets them float off in the brine-clean air.
Nothing of special interest to him.

He is used to finding fragments left by animals
the rest of us hardly ever see. "Catch them back for me"
I say and as he places them in my hand — does this happen
because I have the audacity to love what belongs to wind? —
an eagle descends into the field awkwardly.
Thick black pool of blood congealed behind its right wing.

Shot for sport. Shot for such fierce soaring.
Shot by the hunter, earth-stranded, who weeps
in the late night whiskey-inferno
because he cannot rise above the mountains the way
that god-damned bird does easy as breathing.
I blink again. Field, gone. My sweet blond twin

who caught the feathers back from wind, vanished.
The bird, still there, but skinned. As if my blinking
had pushed past external wound to see within.
Structure of what was, still visible through all the blood.
The eagle trying to use remnants of a wing
to wrap and hide the ruined body but nothing now can be

hidden. You, who so easily carried lightning back to earth
in your gold talons, will die slowly and in pain so fierce
it cannot be named. The intention: to remove
everything you ever loved. Field, wind, shining
dusk, even the star-soaked dark mountain.
And that has been done.

DEATH

When I got there
it was very quiet. Late afternoon.
The porch, empty.
Everyone had gone home.
I slept for awhile in my mother's deep song
of exhaustible sun then woke
just before the first cool air
blew out the green lamps
of the enormous summer trees.

THE WHOLE WEIGHT OF IT

I say goodbye and insects so ancient a pharaoh
could name them
scissor through my insomnia.
Blue locusts with a hunger long as lightning
devour this cache of grain
meant to sustain me
in the after-life.

When I say goodbye, you can't hear, do not
even suspect, talking and
talking, a lock
and a door,
while the tiny key made of sunlight
sinks into the watery gloss
of the passing hearse.

A leafless forest roots here, branches hung
with rags
of ripped-apart nests while the drunk philosopher
expounds the color out of everything —
moss, crow, sun, stone — all gone
grey. His incantation,
"Supposed to be
this way."

Gone, the shell a hermit crab
crawls into. Those enormous blue chambers,
clean streams running through the moon-tiled rooms.
Wind bequeathing to you
and to me all the breath
the dead no longer have need of,
hallowed by sandlewood

and whatever words I am able to make
audible now. Goodbye to the school
of minnows you conjured from a lake by sheer desire
and let them live
in air. Bodies of light
like animate needles
that might have mended us, different

as ocean and oxygen, into an element
we both could share.
You change the living fish
into shocks of light that shine from cups, mirrors,
auto fenders, pliers, saying,
"For you, when I am no longer able
to be here."

Goodbye like a child's paper boat,
poorly constructed.
The bank of the lake growing dark.
No wind crossing the still water.
Fragile vessel beginning
to falter; the whole weight
of sunset is on you.

HAVING BECOME AWARE OF CERTAIN THINGS, I

know who you are. Cloud
of rain drenched grackles. Old derelict
in a grieving coat. Gravedigger.

Or to be fair, let's say you are a hive
so liquid with honey the sun
melts out of lust. But it's all the same

to me as I walk away into the cold
wind wearing gloves of meteorites,
socks of desert sunrise.

Whether or not you remember
my name, I have made a rosary of rain
to pray the roots awake.

Whether or not you have ever
loved me, I levitate in a christening gown
of bonfire.

Whether or not you would look at me
in passing, I am passing
in a wind of bees,

in a wind of the white dresses,
in the wind lean as nobody's dog
shadowy at the road's red edge.

THE GATE

I tell you not to come into my dream anymore
because what is the use of that
when in the world you are as aloof
as a gray gate swinging open, closed, caught
in the wind of whatever happens to have just passed by?

The next night you are not here,
like a stick of incense burned down to dust,
though its remaining fragrance
leaves the address of foreign gardens
lingering a long time in the labyrinth. Deeper in, I am still

trapped in a coffin-sized cubicle, forced to turn
some kind of gear, a wheel. Low drone
of the Invisible Lords of the Perfect Machine hiss
this into place, promising —

You are making the sun rise
somewhere else. What you do drops a coin of light
into a mad person's dark cup, wakes a child from death.
So I drag the implacable wheel
in grief that only deepens, in darkness that only thickens,
believing as I have always believed, the lie

until tonight when the scent, for a second only, of jasmine
brings the garden in and I realize how close the door
has always been. Without thinking, I am through it, I am
running in blue air, on grass as soft as the light
before I entered the house of my mother's body.

The Lords of the Empire of the Perfect Machine
send a tiger after me
first dropping it on a floor of fire,

wanting every leap it makes to be bright with crazy rage.
This is the only light the wheel loves.
The tiger races for me, shadow to the body

it must reach and ruin or never live again.
I say the names of those I love so I may die
in the naming but this tiger
on charred paws is no different from me as it dreams
itself free into blue air, onto grass soft as the light

from before it was born.
For a hundred years, for ten thousand years
it has been running: wind
to word, self to other, red animal of the holy earth,
and reaching me, it leans into me,

light as a life emptied of rage. I remember a river-voice
telling me once how a human soul in danger
of annihilation may be granted the liberty
of shifting shape. Selfless wind of the endangered
garden. A dancing not even fire could devour.

Gray gate swaying slowly open. And beyond that,
someone bending to heal burned hands in a singing river.
Also, a woman, the hem of her night gown, moss-green
and heavy from wading in the water. Low over it all,
sign language of the sunrise clouds, untranslatable.

LAKE MEADOW SKY

It was only after I lost what I loved most,
saw it disappear as surely

as a fish feels the weight of water being pulled away
from its body, too terrified to give credence to the cold
hook buried deep in its throat

that I, weightless in the skyward arc, knew
I would have to love everything.

GOOD, I SAID

Got them home — lace-up, black,
high-heeled. Walked in them
and knew what I had done.
Couldn't take a step
without holding my breath
they hurt so much.

Good, I said, I deserve this
for loving a married man,
for paying,
in the first place,
one hundred fifty two dollars
for a pair of shoes.

I wore them until I had
no memory of how
it even started.
To look at me
you would not have known
a thing was wrong.

I moved with grace.
I said, until it was inbred,
"Surely, in time,
this will become bearable,"
breath held
in a hobble. Seven years.

Until today.
February 1989, the 23rd.
Ground frozen. Snow predicted.
The litany that kept them

laced: *You paid for this.*
You paid.

No matter how big
the mistake, you have to keep
what you bring home.
But this time, I heard.
Right there on the street,
right then

I unlaced them
and took them off, placed them
side by side
and walked away.
I looked back once
and there they were,

stricken, shrunken.
Me, I turned toward home
my feet cold but comfortable
in three dollar
cotton socks,
the color, azure.

RETURNED WHOLE AND WILLING
for Kathleen Romaine

Because you are thousands of miles away
Because there is no one where you are I am sending this
for you and you alone I am leaving

white space here like tundra for the arctic fox to shelter in
expanse and camouflage For you to tell the story as it happened
to you Even from this distance I can hear

As you asked I will listen to every word How you know
even though we were told he was found right away
you know

he died earlier and lay alone in the house on the edge
of the hill with the furnace clicking on and off and his two dogs
whom he loved more I think than he loved us

roaming the house waiting for him to wake and feed them walk
them
to the ocean but he never did

I am starting to tell your story and that's not what this is for

Go on now wherever you are and say how it was

I am listening like wind lifting some small flock
of migrating birds south toward sun and food and a green resting
place

Say what you need to say until it's all out
the way
a drum beat can make you step over the edge of exhaustion not
into dance

exactly but maybe
to a comfortable chair

Say what you need to say until you are as clean as a summer
fountain

I will carry every last word you speak like a cup of water
through desert

like an injured heron that with care can be given back to sky
like the body of our father that I did carry all ash in a metal bottle
what was left of him
and I put him in the earth I remember doing that
though the weight

is still in my hands When I wave to the moon I am wearing
gloves of stone but I wave anyway because I've read
that's where the dead go for awhile

to the moon
and just in case it's true it seems important
to send some sort of signal even if it's very small even
if it's not noticed

I am listening And when you are finished

I will walk you as you asked to your room and settle you
safely in like the father who could not do this
and I will sing
you to sleep

So you will recognize it
when you hear it the music will sound
like ordinary things That is the way I will have to do it
from so far away

Listen for me in the phone that rings once and then stops
In the silence after that I start the song

that is two dogs romping at the edge of blue ocean

A white feather brushing your cheek as its carried along
on invisible currents Listen.

for me in rain nourishing
invisible gardens on the roof I will sing from when

I was lost and mistook for scorched sand
what was after all
the light-filled plateau of a sunflower's face I will sing you
this

4
SOME KISSES

WHY SOME PEOPLE WORSHIP POTATOES
for John Lofty

There are more than you might think —
potato worshipers. They laugh
like dusk in roadside trees as sun sinks
into earth conveying all the salty rumors
from above ground down:
sky-braille of the ferris wheel,
bouquet of roses from a murdered girl's blood,
even the erotic arch of the rainbow
anchoring itself down where the potato
rocks and swells peacefully in its blind ocean,
fat little root-lit Buddha, turning — for love
of above ground flowers
it has never seen — darkness
into harvest.

THE ANGEL IN THE CEREAL BOX
for Spike LaRocca

You told me how the angel had arrived, originally,
piece by piece, in cereal boxes
and I picture it but with difficulty
since she would have been unrecognizable
for several months, rising daily
from crayon-colored boxes of bran and oats.

Blue scrap of skirt, wafer of a hand flattened
in prayer, the small O of her mouth open in song,
all resembling nothing, until you pieced her together,
glued her to plywood. Life-sized, her gaze
clear as any mystic but very young, a child gloriously swamped
in her mother's blue ball gown.

Born, held breathless in a Catholic family. No wonder,
Michael, it was the body itself you fought
so hard to love, your own and the acethylene-souled bodies
of other men. When you left for San Francisco,
that town delirious with edge-of-the-world fireworks,
you gave me the angel, changed your name

to Spike then wrote of how you were finally dancing
in feathers, in the gawdy halo of the shaken tamborine,
in the deep sweet spice of community. Stripping
in gay bars, sequins all over your body. Aware
even then of the way a body, healthy or not, makes
a boundary between your self and the other, whom you loved.

I could not have guessed that you, who had split
the awful black egg of isolation, here, in New Hampshire,

to emerge in California, fierce as a phoenix, would return
at thirty nine, to die. Your family, turning quickly
from the coffin while the high gloss of it still shone
above ground. Then the gravediggers, who had been idling

their trucks behind a long line of cypresses
roared in. No shovels. Just flat-beds, bulldozers,
all the machinery that makes death look easy. But that angel,
paper girl, still stands sweet in my living room,
proof that more often than not it takes time
for the whole picture to come together. Earth: new, wet

unsettled over you. Everywhere, cut flowers in buckets
without water. Then, as if summoned from the invisible
hive, a glory of bees, a sequin-scattering of them
and how like grace, the way they appeared at all, in winter,
and how wholly they gave themselves to the pollen
at the heart of the ruined flowers.

STRAUSS AND THE COWS OF IRELAND

From my room at dusk I watch
the cows in their late graze.
Great clouds of gnats hang over
them, gauzy as a bride's bouquet.
Downstairs, a radio.
Soprano's aria swells
so delicate and pure
it must be unrequited love
but just what the opera is
I can't tell from here,
though later learn: Strauss,
Der Rosenkavalier.
Cows continue to drift
the dusky pasture, luminous,
as if fed on candle-light
instead of grass. They pass
with heavy gentleness, now
and then stopping to lean toward
our windows with little regard
for human arias that reach them
though it conducts
through me a sweetness:
distant opera and the wandering
of star-tiaraed cows in darkness.

MY FRIEND, LOST TO ME IN THE WORLD, RETURNS IN A DREAM

When I finally find you again,
you cannot see me. Your eyes, closed.
The lids, dark, as if bruised.
I ask if you are blind.

"Maybe just tired of looking," you say
and I do not know if this is the truth
or an evasion — the way the Zen master, suffering
a heart attack

tells his disciple, "Do not worry.
It is only my heart singing."
You sit at a table, arms outstretched
as if sifting through the emptiness
for obstacles.

Do you know? Underneath your palms,
in an old clay pot,
in earth
that's dull and dry
from overplanting, somehow

seedlings green as fern,
as koto music stream up
through all the emptiness there ever was
on their string-thin stems
toward your hands.

That is the dream. All there is:
your weariness. Hope opening greenly.
The fear there will be fatal
collisons. Later, awake

I think of the darkness
you must be living in
that is also mine
since it was, after all, my dream.
Darkness like the egg

blown empty but still intact
into which an artisan
crafts a whole jeweled village,
gardens, even citizens,
you kneeling there, lightly

gathering water,
washing your hands
at the fountain that uncurls leaf-green
from the deepest part
of the secret self.

A LITTLE BIT OF TIMELY ADVICE

Time you
put on blue
shoes, high-
heeled, sequined, took
yourself out
dancing.

You been
spending too
much time crying
salty dead-fish lakes
into soup
spoons,

holding
look-alike
contests with doom. Baby,
you need to be moving. Ruin
ruins itself, no
use unplanting

what's left
of your garden. Crank up
the old radio into lion-
looking-for-food
music; or harmonica,

all indigo, breathing up
sunrise. Down and
out's just another

opinion on
up and over.

You say
you got no
makings for
a song? Sing anyway. Best
music's the stuff comes
rising out of nothing.

IN THIS MOMENT

Geranium, broken
by the housepainter's boot,
still forces open one white blossom.

Or the stranger in the blue Chrysler,
a prism hanging
from his rear view mirror

who stops me while I'm dog-walking.
Front teeth missing, he says,
"Come closer.

I won't bite.
I'd just like to take you
out to dinner."

I lie on the hot summer lawn thinking
about this
eat or be eaten world,

blossoms too fragile
to do more than falter.
That's when two women,

eager as talent scouts
or animal trainers, approach.
"May we speak with you concerning God?"

And suddenly, I'm flanked,
sentence fragment
in a big parenthesis.

They're lily of the valley
scented; one's quiet, moral
support; the other's a high pitched

aviary of dark
plumed answers. "You do believe
in God. And hope to get to heaven.

But just what do you
think God thinks of you? Well,
we are here to tell you.

You are, by your mortal
nature, lazy, selfish, untrustworthy,
weak. And do you know

what punishment you deserve
for all your sins?"
I could but do not say

Sin's simply an old archery term
that means to miss the mark
and the ground, ladies, is littered

with your well-meant but
dull arrows. Great sheets of sun
sweep the newly mown lawn and one bird

with a black breast beseeches us to try
any kind of song as it flies
from its high invisible branch

just this once. I love
these ladies in their flower-print
dresses, their Bibles bathed

in the enormous darkness
of their pocketbooks, trying to save
me, from what? I don't

know. Maybe the toothless man
in his blue car full
of rainbows, the severed

branch that still blooms or
the branch that breaks and stays
broken, all

of us unsaved, partial
and as lovely in this
moment as we will ever be.

SOME KISSES

*

Shooting star — that spine of light — sudden in darkness.
The lost child starting its search
for the body grief robbed it of.
This kiss, the abandoned body
returned whole.

*

A kiss as gold and clumsy and glad
as the way tubas
woo wind through Sousa marches.

*

Rivers spangled with the mystery
every explorer has bequeathed to deep water.

*

Blissful as a statue's secret gulping of meteors
the moment after the preoccupied human
has passed.

*

A kiss like a name carved
on an old gravestone, filled in with moss.
From loss, summer
starting its green territories again.

*

Blue-grey of a heron folding itself
into the monastary of the estuary; this kiss, how it feels
to have its solitude fill your body
with love from the necessary
invisible ocean.

*

Kisses that touch you the way the symphony
conductor's hands make love
to music's body.

*

A kiss that loves you the way a telescope loves starlight.

*

Kiss for the part of you hopeless
as the suicide who steps off the bridge into an abyss
that fills quickly with the flat slam of water
black as your mother's anger. No choice
but to give in to this. The letting go. The failing.
Then something small, impossible begins
to happen, just enough
wing to hold you. This kiss
opening.

*

After talking to a woman you once loved,
who did not, I think, love you, you found a rock
in a shopping center parking lot.
"It had been run over alot," you said. "It didn't want
to be run over anymore."

And you took the stone to a small stream
where water in one long kiss covered it and kept
kissing. This is for you, all these kisses
that know how it feels
to take the unbearable weight
of such heavy machinery bearing down over and over.
Then nothing.

A kiss
like the water you put that stone in, water
that is a kind of weeping, not just for the loss
of the woman, whoever she was, but for all of it,
the unspeakable.
Water like love that doesn't change
the stone, wear it down or carry it away. Just touches it.
That's all. Touches it.

DREAMING SPACE AWAKE

For awhile, the mailman stashes Zane Grey and Louis L'Amour
in his mail sack and in each short stretch
between apartments, squirrels and winter-weary shrubs —
he reads a fenceless, stateless, still-forested America back

into place. Between your house and mine,
whole Montana prairies dappled with wild horses.
Halfway to the marine-green mail holding box,
a Lakota Sioux behind a pine, shy

as the wing-singing of returning swans you half-hear
through thick, housed-in sleep. The Government
slow to catch on, finally informs the mailman it's illegal to read
on the job. So he goes farther back

than wild west to first west and now he carries
in his raw, rough satchel, the mail, of course,
but also dozens of tiny plastic dinosaurs he gives to kids
and sometimes me. Just yesterday, a grey stegosaurus

delivered with the electric bill. There's more
than overdue notices being delivered here, more
than catalogues or grocery deals. Between my house
and yours, huge blue beasts from the beginning

link up the entire neighborhood just as easily
as electrical wires and their transformers
or the 3 a.m. dreams that make roads we all meet on,
dance down and waking, erase

while the mailman, day after day, keeps walking,
a weather-blessed tumbleweed seeding in among us
the living corsage of the explorer's campfire,
native peoples shape-shifting

into stone and tree, the pterodactyl's leathery wings
alot more like a mail sack than you might think,
the almost imperceptible breeze alive with the deep slow heave
of the earliest animals, their fern-drenched dreams.

5
TREE

THE TREE OF LIFE

1.
Marriage over. The house taken
by the bank as well as an acre
of small forest. I dreamed
a Northern dusk that never
grew into final dark.
A woman like me, though no sorrow
in her, calm as photology
in the pine's uppermost needle,
guided us both through
bird-thick fern and copper beech.
Air had in it the calm cows leave
after grazing a pasture
and the trees pressed
gentle against our passing:
ancestors eager for word
of distant wayward children.
Small bodies of light
whirled through the dark
like fireflies but more animate —
the trill and warble
of spring-mad orioles. "Angels,"
my guide said, calmly,
"and you may stay here
as long as you like."

2.
It was not the breaking
of the law that troubled me, host
of lawyers dissembling marriage vows,
nor even the loss of a house
embedded in forest, like forest itself.
Wind pressed to each part of it

in the continual embrace of belonging.
You see, this much into the telling
and still I have not mentioned
husband. We belonged, a union odd
and endearing as the lucent skins
an onion wraps itself in, many selves
shining as one. I lost the world
in that undoing.

3.
Left to its natural course,
a river — at obvious rock —
simply diverts in another direction.
But I mistook the stone
for a place to stop and hung there
dumb as an unstrung harp, bruised
into the long monotone of *no*
by self-imposed, obdurate dark.
To put it more clearly, I drank.

4.
Half a bottle every evening —
as passport, reward, a holiday abroad —
for having navigated the world. I invited
oblivion in the smallest hours
and then denied it by daylight despite
my body still hanging from the shining
black hook of the meat packer's fancy —
Maker's Mark whiskey,
Old Crow or *Four Roses.*

5.
Husband. You appear
thin and dying, unable
to walk, except for a crutch
that shakes with a whole
nation's famine. You, once
my lover, now unexplainably
scarecrow's brother.
Inside a hive of stone
you die. They lay you
in a boat of white satin.
Face pressed to the pillow
you look almost young
in limitless breath-starved
rest. The undertaker, drunk,
heaves another body
beside you. He's angry
you died in debt, wants
you to pay by sharing
death. You startle awake
too weary to climb out
of the coffin, call
my name but as I stretch
my hand to help you,
you shrink back
into vagrant's cradle,
skin splotched as wet flour,
wrapped tight
in a swaddling of howl.

6.
The wall between waking and sleep,
thick. To circumvent it, I've fallen
into the habit of inventing: lie
prisoner on a foreign planet.
My captors, self-deceived, believe
me sovereign in the home I've abandoned.
And so even alien, I'm seen
as suitable chattel for their King.
A kind of *corporeal movable,* identified
by the King's cats who will nuzzle
only royalty and choose to nest with me.
Thus worthy, but not entitled to the rights
of citizenship, I lie in this strange bed
while hooded women bring linens,
scissors, blue eggs and perfume.
And the moon-calf King, already husband
a hundred times over whirls
through the palace in a rage of red robes.
As always, a quiet woman waits,
the patience of trees in her, her cloak —
the rich brown of earth newly turned
for planting — no hood to hide
her gentle face or the clear glass beads
as full of light as fireflies
that encircle, in diadem, her unbent head.
I could give my hand to her
and be released both from the grief
that haunts me in this fantasy
or harms me in waking
but it is always just before I reach
my hand to her that I lose consciousness
or faith and falter into drunken sleep.

7.
When the human cerebellum
is cut in half vertifcally
the pattern of a tree reveals itself
titled, scientifically,
arbor vitae, the tree of life,
also found in Eden.

8.
I wait in late summer dark
for the galaxy of hooded women, healer
and intoxicated King
when my dog jumps up on the bed
and settles on the other, never-used pillow.
He stares out the window
as if some form of canine theater
were occuring there just for his pleasure.
This evening, a rare one,
I'm sober, tranquil enough to turn over
for a dog's eye view of things
although I suspect all I'll see:
obscurity, moon-starved autumn.

9.
Young maple, allayed to summer green
but harvest stain of yellow in it, too.
That much, clear. Then wind directed me
to one dark leaf. A long look later
it became a map to all interior regions,
a measure of how far the tree would grow
to reach equilibrium, peaceful, slow.
Wind and leaves began to mesh.
Though separate as to form — something

invisible entered in — showed them
as one: maple and air, married skin
to skin, close as wave to ocean, clearly kin.

10.
Glittery as the aerial view one gets
of city streets at night
from a plane in holding pattern,
tributaries of light began to flow
from leaf to trunk through root
and up again — what human blood must do
from heart to limb — sap blossoming
easily to even the farthest artery.
I drank it in.

11.
One way is to invent a life
in outer space to survive
what's eating away at the inner.
Another is to pay attention
at the open window.

12.
I could see the sound of bells,
animate, corporeal among the branches
like tiny moths of match flame drawn
to candle's wick, exactly like the angels
of the *you-may-stay-here* dream.
This was an ordinary evening
in New Hampshire, simple
maple, solid trunk and bark,
the lighter leaves and buried

chapel of the roots
exactly equal. Years later
and still that vision lends itself
to heal a daily lack of faith, the tree
quietly mending the void
between what I want and what is,
root and wing. In the beginning
and after that, no edge
or end to anything.

CONTENTS OF A BREATH ABOUT TO BE EXHALED
AS *'I LOVE YOU'*

All the way this
wind has travelled to me — from romancing
a child's tattered white kite,

from carrying for burial
unto heaven the black bowler of the banker, the begonia-
hearted money lender,

from marrying laundry-line-shirts
to sky
in civil ceremony,

having smacked the slack sail of a galleon
through the horizon's blue loop-hole.
All the way

from the shallow lungs of a lamb
that later was slaughtered —
this breath that stopped only once to perfume itself

in the spindly garden of an old woman
harvesting snapdragons and wild onions
for her salad of flame,

the wind that at midnight combs the manes
of becalmed carousel animals —
gives lift to the hand just letting go of the trapeze,

to the firefly,
to the ghost of the snowy egret. Easing, then,
its admissable evidence across the cheek

of the one lying awake late
in a cocoon of tears thinking no one knows but I
know. Let it all go as wind, *I*,

assembles the first clouds of summer, *love*,
the tree pushing through boulder to light its green
chandelier of leaves, you. Just *you.* *You.*